HAVE YOU EVER?

Have You Ever?

391 questions to help you know yourself and others

by Anna Van Evera

Boston ♦ Alyson Publications, Inc.

Published by Alyson Publications, Inc.,
40 Plympton Street, Boston, Massachusetts 02118.
Distributed in England by GMP Publishers, P.O. Box 247, London N17 9QR, England.

First Alyson edition: May 1994
An earlier version, titled *Getting to Know You,* was published by the author in 1992.

1 3 5 4 2

ISBN 1-55583-257-1

ACKNOWLEDGEMENTS

Many thanks to all the women that I have known and dealt with throughout my life, for it is from these experiences that this book arose. In particular, I want to thank my lover, Mary Anne Mirek, and our housemate, Colleen Kelley, for their invaluable input and support in this endeavor. During the course of creating this book, we laughed and cried and learned a lot about ourselves and each other. In the end, we believe everything we learned is well worth knowing.

If you have comments, I would be happy to hear from you. Please direct correspondence to me, in care of Alyson Publications, 40 Plympton Street, Boston, MA 02118.

INTRODUCTION

Many people in this culture have trouble communicating. Though social conditioning may make it especially hard for boys and men to express themselves, most of us know that difficulty with communicating, especially with a partner, is not strictly a gender issue.

What follows here is a variety of questions, statements, and hypothetical scenarios. Although specifically compiled to help facilitate communication between lesbian partners, this book can be used by anyone who is in a relationship or who wants to explore a range of topics. Those of you who have already discussed many of these issues can use it as an opportunity to reiterate your feelings and note any changes that time and circumstance may have brought to your relationship.

I believe that all of the issues in this book are important to think about, talk about, and share our feelings about. I believe that if you read through this book and respond honestly to the material, you will learn things about yourself that need knowing. And going through *Have You Ever* with a partner will open communication, and should strengthen the relationship. If you find yourself unable to respond to any of the questions, I suggest that you make a list of the items that make you the most uncomfortable. These items will serve as personal "danger markers" for you and point out issues you may wish to examine more thoroughly.

How you choose to read this book is up to you. You may decide to quickly skim through the questions, responding with just one word or not responding at all. But if you take the time and effort to respond thoughtfully and thoroughly, it could prove invaluable to you, whether or not you are presently involved in a partnership.

I sincerely hope that this book will stimulate honest introspection, helping you to see which doors you have closed and which doors you have open. Each of us is unique. We take different paths and have different rates of growth. We all have fears and joys. Let this book serve as a means to illuminate more clearly what your path is and how your fears and joys operate in your life.

Have You Ever makes for lively party entertainment. But some of you may also want to go through the book item by item, writing or taping your responses. After making note of your responses, consult the appendix in the back of the book. This appendix lists item numbers that relate loosely to three specific areas. Close review of your responses to these items could reveal possible problems in, or at least a need for a closer look at, these areas. Your responses may or may not indicate that you might benefit from professional consultation. Keep in mind that seeking therapeutic consultation is not indicative of any failure. It is simply gathering information from a source that has access to a larger body of knowledge and resources. The more information that each of us can gather about any issue, the broader our base, and the greater our possible array of options. For those of us who are seeking options, formal counseling can be an excellent source.

Have fun with this material. The responses you hear may delight and surprise, as well as inform. When viewed with a balance of seriousness and humor, *Have You Ever* could be a source that you and yours will refer to again and again. Enjoy!

◆◆◆◆◆◆◆◆◆◆◆◆◆

1. *I*f you could have three wishes right now, what would they be?

◆◆◆◆◆◆◆◆◆◆◆◆◆

2. *W*hat is the most planning you have ever put into a romantic event? Was it worth it?

◆◆◆◆◆◆◆◆◆◆◆◆◆

3. *I*n picking a life partner, would you follow your head or your heart?

◆◆◆◆◆◆◆◆◆◆◆◆◆◆

4. *I*s there any one place where you find it easier to have important talks with your lover, such as in the car or in bed?

◆◆◆◆◆◆◆◆◆◆◆◆◆◆

5. *W*hen a couple breaks up, does it mean that one of the partners has failed?

◆◆◆◆◆◆◆◆◆◆◆◆◆◆

6. *C*an people be in love with each other even if they don't strive to stay together as permanent partners?

◆◆◆◆◆◆◆◆◆◆◆◆◆◆◆

7. **A**s a child, did you ever have to care for, nurture, or "parent" one of your parents? If so, how do you feel about that?

◆◆◆◆◆◆◆◆◆◆◆◆◆◆

8. **H**ow long does it take a couple to work things out between them? One year, two, three, more?

◆◆◆◆◆◆◆◆◆◆◆◆◆◆

9. **D**o you think that more lesbians have cats or have dogs as pets?

♦♦♦♦♦♦♦♦♦♦♦♦♦♦

10. *T*rue or false: When my partner is happy, I am happy.

♦♦♦♦♦♦♦♦♦♦♦♦♦♦

11. *D*o you think the phrase "I love you" means more or less to you than it does to your lover? Your friends? What does it mean to you to be in love?

♦♦♦♦♦♦♦♦♦♦♦♦♦♦

12. *W*hen you're unhappy, do you feel hurt if your lover doesn't go out of her way try to cheer you up?

◆◆◆◆◆◆◆◆◆◆◆◆◆◆

13. **W**ould you describe your lover as a good listener?

◆◆◆◆◆◆◆◆◆◆◆◆◆◆

14. **D**escribe the last time you felt your lover really listened to you. Describe the last time you felt your lover really *didn't* listen to you.

◆◆◆◆◆◆◆◆◆◆◆◆◆◆◆

15. **W**ould you be more comfortable talking to an ex-lover at a party with or without your present lover standing with you? Why?

◆◆◆◆◆◆◆◆◆◆◆◆◆◆

16. **D**o you sometimes fantasize or wish that your lover would do a certain thing in bed or act a certain way? Would you be afraid to tell her for fear that she would think you didn't like things as they are now? *Do* you like things as they are now? Are you ashamed of some of your fantasies?

◆◆◆◆◆◆◆◆◆◆◆◆◆◆

17. *D*o you feel safe talking about specific sexual behaviors and techniques with your lover? Friends? Family?

◆◆◆◆◆◆◆◆◆◆◆◆◆◆

18. *A*gree or disagree: Real lesbians don't use dildos.

♦♦♦♦♦♦♦♦♦♦♦♦♦♦

19. **D**oes your lover let you know what she wants during sex? If so, how?

♦♦♦♦♦♦♦♦♦♦♦♦♦♦

20. **D**o you ever feel as though she is "correcting" you?

♦♦♦♦♦♦♦♦♦♦♦♦♦♦

21. **H**as your lover ever criticized your sexual technique? If so, how did you take it?

◆◆◆◆◆◆◆◆◆◆◆◆◆◆

22. *A*re there unspoken steps that you and your lover follow during sex?

◆◆◆◆◆◆◆◆◆◆◆◆◆◆

23. *W*hich of you usually initiates sex? Does the initiator usually follow through? If you initiate sex, do you prefer immediate reciprocation? If your lover initiates sex, does she prefer immediate reciprocation? Do each of you usually expect the other to reciprocate?

◆◆◆◆◆◆◆◆◆◆◆◆◆◆

24. **W**hat signals do you use to indicate that you'd like to be sexual?

◆◆◆◆◆◆◆◆◆◆◆◆◆◆

25. **N**ame two things your lover does or says
to let you know she wants to get sexual.

◆◆◆◆◆◆◆◆◆◆◆◆◆◆

26. **D**o you ever ask your lover to make love to you? Does
she ever say no? Why or why not? Have you ever said no
to your lover? Why or why not? Would you feel hurt if your
lover said no?

◆◆◆◆◆◆◆◆◆◆◆◆◆◆

27. **D**o you think the frequency of sex changes throughout a relationship?

◆◆◆◆◆◆◆◆◆◆◆◆◆◆

28. **D**o you pay attention to how often you have sex?

◆◆◆◆◆◆◆◆◆◆◆◆◆

29. **D**oes your lover pay attention to how often you have sex?

◆◆◆◆◆◆◆◆◆◆◆◆◆◆◆

30. *D*o you ever react in ways you don't expect during sex?

◆◆◆◆◆◆◆◆◆◆◆◆◆◆◆

31. *I*f your lover asked you to do something in bed that you found distasteful, would you try it anyway or just refuse?

◆◆◆◆◆◆◆◆◆◆◆◆◆◆◆

32. *H*ave you and your lover spoken specifically and graphically about sexual positions, styles, preferences?

♦♦♦♦♦♦♦♦♦♦♦♦♦♦

33. **D**o you like to make noise during sex?

♦♦♦♦♦♦♦♦♦♦♦♦♦♦

34. **D**o you like your lover to make noise during sex?

♦♦♦♦♦♦♦♦♦♦♦♦♦♦

35. **D**o you and your lover have a safe word?

♦♦♦♦♦♦♦♦♦♦♦♦♦♦

36. **D**o you like spontaneous sex?

◆◆◆◆◆◆◆◆◆◆◆◆◆◆

37. **H**ow well do you adapt to changes in your sexual behavior?

◆◆◆◆◆◆◆◆◆◆◆◆◆◆

38. **D**o you enjoy being vaginally penetrated?
With one finger, two, more?

◆◆◆◆◆◆◆◆◆◆◆◆◆◆

39. **D**o you enjoy vaginally penetrating your lover?

♦♦♦♦♦♦♦♦♦♦♦♦♦♦

40. **D**o you like feeling your lover's tongue in your vagina?

♦♦♦♦♦♦♦♦♦♦♦♦♦♦

41. **D**o you like feeling your lover's tongue in your anus?

♦♦♦♦♦♦♦♦♦♦♦♦♦♦

42. **I**f something is painful during sex, do you react immediately or do you wait to see if your partner stops on her own before saying anything?

♦♦♦♦♦♦♦♦♦♦♦♦♦♦

43. *H*ave you ever been tied up during sex?

♦♦♦♦♦♦♦♦♦♦♦♦♦♦

44. *D*o you think sex is something that doesn't need to be talked about if it's done enough, done right, and you're in love?

♦♦♦♦♦♦♦♦♦♦♦♦♦

45. *N*ame one thing that each of your ex-lovers would never do in bed. Why not?

◆◆◆◆◆◆◆◆◆◆◆◆◆◆

46. *N*ame at least one thing that *you* would never do in bed. Why not?

◆◆◆◆◆◆◆◆◆◆◆◆◆◆

47. *D*o you feel that masturbation is something to do only when one does not have a sex partner?

◆◆◆◆◆◆◆◆◆◆◆◆◆◆

48. *D*o you masturbate? Have you ever masturbated in front of a lover? What if she asked you to do so?

♦♦♦♦♦♦♦♦♦♦♦♦♦♦

49. **D**oes your lover masturbate?
Has she ever done so in front of you?
Would you want her to?

♦♦♦♦♦♦♦♦♦♦♦♦♦♦♦

50. **H**ow would you feel if you came home
unexpectedly and found your lover masturbating?

♦♦♦♦♦♦♦♦♦♦♦♦♦

51. **D**o you always work toward orgasm for your partner
when you make love?

◆◆◆◆◆◆◆◆◆◆◆◆◆◆

52. **D**o you always work toward orgasm
when you make love to yourself?

◆◆◆◆◆◆◆◆◆◆◆◆◆◆

53. **D**o you apologize if your lover doesn't reach orgasm?

◆◆◆◆◆◆◆◆◆◆◆◆◆◆

54. **I**s your lover disappointed if she doesn't reach orgasm?

◆◆◆◆◆◆◆◆◆◆◆◆◆◆

55. *A*re you disappointed if your lover doesn't reach orgasm?

◆◆◆◆◆◆◆◆◆◆◆◆◆◆

56. *D*oes your lover get angry or upset with you
if she doesn't reach orgasm?

◆◆◆◆◆◆◆◆◆◆◆◆◆◆

57. *D*o you enjoy being anally penetrated?
Do you enjoy anally penetrating a lover?

◆◆◆◆◆◆◆◆◆◆◆◆◆◆

58. **D**o you like to play with sex toys?

◆◆◆◆◆◆◆◆◆◆◆◆◆◆

59. **H**ave you ever used food for sex play?

◆◆◆◆◆◆◆◆◆◆◆◆◆◆

60. **H**ave you ever used a special dinner as a prelude to sex?

◆◆◆◆◆◆◆◆◆◆◆◆◆

61. **D**o you think using sexual aids or toys can be addictive?

♦♦♦♦♦♦♦♦♦♦♦♦♦♦

62. **H**ave you ever used a dildo? Have you ever wanted to?

♦♦♦♦♦♦♦♦♦♦♦♦♦♦

63. **D**o you think that women who use dildos secretly want a man or want to *be* a man? That dildos are only substitute penises?

◆◆◆◆◆◆◆◆◆◆◆◆◆◆

64. **W**ould you be willing to explore being physically restrained during sex?

◆◆◆◆◆◆◆◆◆◆◆◆◆◆

65. **W**ould it make a difference to you how you were restrained? For instance, if your lover simply held your wrists, as opposed to handcuffing or tieing you?

◆◆◆◆◆◆◆◆◆◆◆◆◆◆

66. **I**f you were tied up, would you need the safety feature of a quick release from the bonds?

◆◆◆◆◆◆◆◆◆◆◆◆◆◆

67. **W**ould you be willing to tie your lover up,
even if it isn't something you'd want for yourself?

◆◆◆◆◆◆◆◆◆◆◆◆◆◆

68. *W*ould you be willing to be blindfolded while tied up?

◆◆◆◆◆◆◆◆◆◆◆◆◆◆

69. **W**ould you let your lover take nude snapshots of
you? Would you let someone else photograph the
two of you? Why or why not?

◆◆◆◆◆◆◆◆◆◆◆◆◆◆

70. **W**hen is touching your lover inappropriate? In public? In front of family?

◆◆◆◆◆◆◆◆◆◆◆◆◆◆

71. **W**hen is kissing your lover inappropriate?

◆◆◆◆◆◆◆◆◆◆◆◆◆◆

72. **I**f you and your lover were unable to communicate verbally for as long as a week, how do you think you would get along? What do you think would be the hardest thing about it?

♦♦♦♦♦♦♦♦♦♦♦♦♦♦

73. **H**ave you ever discussed the details of your sex life with anyone besides your lover? How would you feel if you learned that your lover had discussed a sexual problem with one or more of her friends? Would it matter if they were mutual friends?

♦♦♦♦♦♦♦♦♦♦♦♦♦

74. **H**ave you ever been in love with your image of how things could be with someone? If so, were you aware at the time that it was happening? If not, would it have made any difference in the relationship? How so?

◆◆◆◆◆◆◆◆◆◆◆◆◆◆

75. **W**hen somebody you like feels more for you than you do for her, do you push her away for her own good, talk with her about it and let her decide for herself if that's okay, keep it to yourself but don't pretend any great love, or do you do something else entirely? Why?

◆◆◆◆◆◆◆◆◆◆◆◆◆◆

76. **I**f someone asks your lover to play pool, do you feel she is flirting?

◆◆◆◆◆◆◆◆◆◆◆◆◆◆

77. *I*f a woman buys your lover a drink,
do you consider her to be flirting?

◆◆◆◆◆◆◆◆◆◆◆◆◆◆

78. *D*o you think flirting is romantic?

◆◆◆◆◆◆◆◆◆◆◆◆◆◆

79. *D*o you like to flirt?

◆◆◆◆◆◆◆◆◆◆◆◆◆◆

80. *N*ame five things that you do for your lover that you consider to be romantic.

◆◆◆◆◆◆◆◆◆◆◆◆◆◆

81. *N*ame five things that your lover does for you that you consider to be romantic.

◆◆◆◆◆◆◆◆◆◆◆◆◆◆

82. *D*o you agree or disagree: Flirting is fun.

◆◆◆◆◆◆◆◆◆◆◆◆◆◆

83. *F*lirting is scary.

◆◆◆◆◆◆◆◆◆◆◆◆◆◆

84. *F*lirting is risky.

◆◆◆◆◆◆◆◆◆◆◆◆◆◆

85. *D*o you feel flirting by either partner with anyone else is a sign of discontent?

◆◆◆◆◆◆◆◆◆◆◆◆◆◆

86. **D**o you like to watch your lover flirt?

◆◆◆◆◆◆◆◆◆◆◆◆◆◆

87. **D**o you take it as a compliment when someone makes a pass at your lover, or do you get upset?

◆◆◆◆◆◆◆◆◆◆◆◆◆

88. **D**o you agree or disagree:
Flirting is a way to get to know people.

♦♦♦♦♦♦♦♦♦♦♦♦♦♦♦

89. *H*ow would you react, and what would you do, if you thought that someone was trying to break you and your lover apart?

♦♦♦♦♦♦♦♦♦♦♦♦♦♦

90. *A*gree or disagree: Love involves pain.

♦♦♦♦♦♦♦♦♦♦♦♦♦

91. *N*ame three expectations you have of yourself.

◆◆◆◆◆◆◆◆◆◆◆◆◆◆

92. *N*ame one expectation you have of your lover.

◆◆◆◆◆◆◆◆◆◆◆◆◆◆

93. *D*o you ever hit yourself during or just after an argument?

◆◆◆◆◆◆◆◆◆◆◆◆◆◆

94. *H*ave you ever hit someone during an argument?

◆◆◆◆◆◆◆◆◆◆◆◆◆◆

95. **H**ave you ever thrown an object during or just after an argument?

◆◆◆◆◆◆◆◆◆◆◆◆◆◆

96. **H**ave you ever accidentally hit a pet during an argument?

◆◆◆◆◆◆◆◆◆◆◆◆◆◆

97. **H**ave you ever hit a family member during an argument?

◆◆◆◆◆◆◆◆◆◆◆◆◆◆

98. *H*ave you ever hit a stranger or acquaintance during an argument or a fight?

◆◆◆◆◆◆◆◆◆◆◆◆◆◆

99. *D*o you believe that violence cancels out love?

◆◆◆◆◆◆◆◆◆◆◆◆◆◆

100. *D*o you believe it is normal to disagree and to argue?

◆◆◆◆◆◆◆◆◆◆◆◆◆◆

101. **I**s it normal to fight?

◆◆◆◆◆◆◆◆◆◆◆◆◆◆

102. **D**o you know the difference between disagreeing and arguing? Explain.

◆◆◆◆◆◆◆◆◆◆◆◆◆◆

103. **H**ave you ever pushed or shoved your lover during an argument?

◆◆◆◆◆◆◆◆◆◆◆◆◆◆

104. **H**ow important are your lover's needs to you?

◆◆◆◆◆◆◆◆◆◆◆◆◆◆

105. **D**o you think someone who says she's nonmonogamous is incapable of loyalty and commitment?

◆◆◆◆◆◆◆◆◆◆◆◆◆◆

106. **W**ould you read your lover's private journal? Why or why not? What if she gave you permission?

◆◆◆◆◆◆◆◆◆◆◆◆◆◆

107. **D**o you feel unfaithful if you have sexual fantasies about someone other than your lover? Why or why not?

◆◆◆◆◆◆◆◆◆◆◆◆◆◆

108. **W**hat "understandings" between you and your lover are nonnegotiable?

◆◆◆◆◆◆◆◆◆◆◆◆◆◆

109. **W**hat pleases you sexually? What do you enjoy most about having sex?

◆◆◆◆◆◆◆◆◆◆◆◆◆◆

110. **H**ave you learned more about what pleases you from long-term or from short-term partners?

◆◆◆◆◆◆◆◆◆◆◆◆◆◆

111. **D**o you practice safe sex?

◆◆◆◆◆◆◆◆◆◆◆◆◆◆

112. **H**ave you ever gone down on a woman during her period? Would you if you knew she was HIV-positive?

◆◆◆◆◆◆◆◆◆◆◆◆◆◆

113. *I*f you had the power to hear your lover's every thought for one half hour a day, would you use it? Why or why not? When would you use it?

◆◆◆◆◆◆◆◆◆◆◆◆◆◆

114. *W*ould you use it during sex? Why or why not?

◆◆◆◆◆◆◆◆◆◆◆◆◆

115. *W*ould you want your partner to hear your thoughts? Why or why not?

♦♦♦♦♦♦♦♦♦♦♦♦♦♦

116. *A* re there any telltale signals in your relationship that indicate to you that there is something that you and your lover need to work on?

♦♦♦♦♦♦♦♦♦♦♦♦♦♦

117. *N* ame the last three things that you and your lover fought about. Do you often argue about the same things?

♦♦♦♦♦♦♦♦♦♦♦♦♦♦

118. *H* ow long does an argument with your lover usually last?

◆◆◆◆◆◆◆◆◆◆◆◆◆◆

119. **D**o you ever feel that your lover is competing with you? Where? When?

◆◆◆◆◆◆◆◆◆◆◆◆◆◆

120. **N**ame five problem areas in your relationship in order of importance.

♦♦♦♦♦♦♦♦♦♦♦♦♦♦

121. **N**ame three things that you are good at.

♦♦♦♦♦♦♦♦♦♦♦♦♦♦

122. **N**ame three things that you enjoy.

♦♦♦♦♦♦♦♦♦♦♦♦♦♦

123. **N**ame three things that your lover does really well.

♦♦♦♦♦♦♦♦♦♦♦♦♦♦

124. **N**ame three things that she especially enjoys.

◆◆◆◆◆◆◆◆◆◆◆◆◆◆

125. *N*ame three things that you're not so good at, that you think you should work on. Identify one step for each item you can take toward improving.

◆◆◆◆◆◆◆◆◆◆◆◆◆◆

126. *N*ame one step your lover might take to help you reach your goal.

◆◆◆◆◆◆◆◆◆◆◆◆◆◆

127. *N*ame three things you'd like to see your lover work to improve.

◆◆◆◆◆◆◆◆◆◆◆◆◆◆

128. *I*dentify one step you can take for each thing to help her reach her goal.

◆◆◆◆◆◆◆◆◆◆◆◆◆◆

129. **A** gree or disagree: Trust is earned.

◆◆◆◆◆◆◆◆◆◆◆◆◆◆

130. **W** hat is the worst thing that an ex-lover has ever done to you?

◆◆◆◆◆◆◆◆◆◆◆◆◆◆

131. **W** hat is the best thing that an ex-lover has ever done for you?

◆◆◆◆◆◆◆◆◆◆◆◆◆

132. *C*omplete the following sentences
with at least three different items:

◆ Things would be a lot better if only I'd

_____.

◆ Things would be a lot better if only my lover would

_____.

◆◆◆◆◆◆◆◆◆◆◆◆◆

133. *W*hat is the best thing that has happened with your current
lover? What is the worst thing that has happened with your
current lover?

◆◆◆◆◆◆◆◆◆◆◆◆◆◆

134. **H**ave you ever gone to any twelve-step meetings? Did it help? Why or why not?

◆◆◆◆◆◆◆◆◆◆◆◆◆◆

135. **D**id your parents/family/primary caregivers ever say things *to* you or *about* you that hurt you?

◆◆◆◆◆◆◆◆◆◆◆◆◆◆

136. **D**id they ever do things that hurt you either emotionally or physically?

◆◆◆◆◆◆◆◆◆◆◆◆◆◆

137. **D**escribe your best memory from childhood. Describe your worst memory. Describe your scariest memory.

◆◆◆◆◆◆◆◆◆◆◆◆◆◆

138. **N**ame something from your childhood that made you very angry. How does it make you feel now?

◆◆◆◆◆◆◆◆◆◆◆◆◆◆

139. **N**ame at least one thing that you wish each of your parents had done differently when you were growing up.

◆◆◆◆◆◆◆◆◆◆◆◆◆◆

140. **D**id your parents or siblings ever hit you?
Did they ever throw anything at you?

◆◆◆◆◆◆◆◆◆◆◆◆◆◆

141. **W**hat constitutes "average" or "normal" discipline for
a five-year-old? A thirteen-year-old? A sixteen-year-old?

◆◆◆◆◆◆◆◆◆◆◆◆◆

142. **H**ave you ever had sex when you didn't really want to?

♦♦♦♦♦♦♦♦♦♦♦♦♦♦

143. **D**o you consider sex to be an important part of a relationship?

♦♦♦♦♦♦♦♦♦♦♦♦♦♦

144. **D**o you ever see, hear, or feel things during sex that don't seem to fit the circumstances of the moment?

♦♦♦♦♦♦♦♦♦♦♦♦♦

145. **H**ow would you feel if your lover told you she'd like to find out what someone else was like in bed?

◆◆◆◆◆◆◆◆◆◆◆◆◆◆

146. **W**ould you consider your lover disloyal if she were to think about having sex with someone else?

◆◆◆◆◆◆◆◆◆◆◆◆◆◆

147. **W**ould you consider your lover disloyal if she fondly remembers something that happened in bed with an ex-lover?

◆◆◆◆◆◆◆◆◆◆◆◆◆◆

148. **N**ame your favorite thing about sex that occurred with someone other than your present lover.

◆◆◆◆◆◆◆◆◆◆◆◆◆◆

149. **W**hen you are sick and feeling badly, would you rather have your lover with you or not? Why?

◆◆◆◆◆◆◆◆◆◆◆◆◆

150. **A**gree or disagree: Everyone needs to have time alone.

◆◆◆◆◆◆◆◆◆◆◆◆◆◆

151. **W**here was the most unusual place you have ever had sex? Where is the most unusual place you've ever *wanted* to have sex?

◆◆◆◆◆◆◆◆◆◆◆◆◆◆

152. **I**f your lover announced that she was going for a drive alone, would you worry? Why or why not?

◆◆◆◆◆◆◆◆◆◆◆◆◆◆

153. **H**ave you maintained friendships with any former lovers? Why or why not?

◆◆◆◆◆◆◆◆◆◆◆◆◆◆

154. **D**o you ever wish that you had or had not done so?

◆◆◆◆◆◆◆◆◆◆◆◆◆◆

155. *I*f you got flowers and a card from a woman who said she had
a crush on you, would you display them? Why or why not?
How do you think your lover would react?
How would you want your lover to react?

◆◆◆◆◆◆◆◆◆◆◆◆◆◆

156. **W**hich of the following tactics do you use most often
when trying to get your way: intimidating, warning,
coaxing, reasoning, pleading, whining.
Which does your lover use?

◆◆◆◆◆◆◆◆◆◆◆◆◆◆

157. *W*hat was the last really important issue that you and your lover disagreed about? Did you ever resolve the issue? How? Would you like to change the resolution or is it still acceptable?

◆◆◆◆◆◆◆◆◆◆◆◆◆◆

158. *I*f you and your lover were in a room with a squeaky bed and walls so thin you could hear voices from the next room, would you still have sex? Would you make any changes in your lovemaking?

◆◆◆◆◆◆◆◆◆◆◆◆◆◆

159. **D**o you have heart-to-heart talks with your lover? How often? What are they like?

◆◆◆◆◆◆◆◆◆◆◆◆◆◆

160. **D**o you talk mostly to share feelings or to solve problems? Is this how you wish things to remain?

◆◆◆◆◆◆◆◆◆◆◆◆◆◆

161. *I*f your lover suddenly left you, when would you start dating again?

◆◆◆◆◆◆◆◆◆◆◆◆◆◆

162. *W*hat is the longest time that you have spent between lovers? The shortest time?

◆◆◆◆◆◆◆◆◆◆◆◆◆◆

163. *W*ould how quickly you started dating again be influenced by how or why you broke up with your last lover?

◆◆◆◆◆◆◆◆◆◆◆◆◆

164. **D**o you find yourself more attracted to someone who is similar to your ex-lover(s) or different?

◆◆◆◆◆◆◆◆◆◆◆◆◆◆

165. **W**hat are your rules about dating women who have lovers?

◆◆◆◆◆◆◆◆◆◆◆◆◆

166. **W**ould you date a woman who said that she was bisexual? Why or why not?

◆◆◆◆◆◆◆◆◆◆◆◆◆◆

167. **W**ould you date a woman who broke up with her lover last week? Three months ago? A year ago?

◆◆◆◆◆◆◆◆◆◆◆◆◆◆

168. **W**ould you date a woman who said she was straight?

◆◆◆◆◆◆◆◆◆◆◆◆◆◆

169. **H**ow would you feel if you found out the woman you've been dating regularly for a month was seeing other women? Would it make any difference if she were sexual with you? Them?

◆◆◆◆◆◆◆◆◆◆◆◆◆◆

170. **H**ave you ever left someone? Why? Why not?

◆◆◆◆◆◆◆◆◆◆◆◆◆◆

171. **D**o you consider yourself monogamous? Have you had more than one lover?

◆◆◆◆◆◆◆◆◆◆◆◆◆◆

172. **F**or each of your breakups, what or who was the cause?

◆◆◆◆◆◆◆◆◆◆◆◆◆◆

173. **H**ave you ever gone to bed with a woman only once? Why or why not?

◆◆◆◆◆◆◆◆◆◆◆◆◆

174. **D**o you wait until you think someone else is interested in you before you end a relationship? Have you ever done so?

◆◆◆◆◆◆◆◆◆◆◆◆◆

175. **W**hat sort of implicit commitment do you make with someone if you are sexual with her?

◆◆◆◆◆◆◆◆◆◆◆◆◆◆

176. **W**ould you ever date a co-worker? Why or why not?

◆◆◆◆◆◆◆◆◆◆◆◆◆◆

177. **H**ow would you feel if someone you knew was seriously involved with one of your ex-lovers?

◆◆◆◆◆◆◆◆◆◆◆◆◆

178. **W**hat's the longest length of time you felt possessive about an ex-lover?

◆◆◆◆◆◆◆◆◆◆◆◆◆◆

179. **W**ould you describe yourself as a possessive lover?

◆◆◆◆◆◆◆◆◆◆◆◆◆◆

180. **I**f a woman made a pass at you, how would your lover react? How would you want her to react? Would you be upset if she wasn't jealous?

◆◆◆◆◆◆◆◆◆◆◆◆◆◆

181. **W**hich of you seems to need more time apart: you or your partner?

◆◆◆◆◆◆◆◆◆◆◆◆◆◆◆

182. **W**ould you enter into a relationship with someone you loved even if you knew that, regardless of the outcome, you could never be lovers with anyone else again — in other words, if you knew that, whether it worked or not, it would be your last relationship ever?

◆◆◆◆◆◆◆◆◆◆◆◆◆◆◆

183. **D**o you believe that the person who leaves a relationship is the one who is giving up on that relationship?

◆◆◆◆◆◆◆◆◆◆◆◆◆◆

184. ***H*** as any of your lovers ever died?

◆◆◆◆◆◆◆◆◆◆◆◆◆◆

185. ***H*** ave you ever had someone close to you die?
How did you deal with it?

◆◆◆◆◆◆◆◆◆◆◆◆◆◆

186. **H**ave you made a will? Why or why not?

◆◆◆◆◆◆◆◆◆◆◆◆◆◆

187. **W**ould your family contest a will that left everything to your lover? Would she fight them for what is rightfully hers?

◆◆◆◆◆◆◆◆◆◆◆◆◆◆

188. **W**hen you fall in love, do your relationships with your friends change? If so, do you think your friends get upset?

♦♦♦♦♦♦♦♦♦♦♦♦♦♦♦

189. **H**ow would you react if your partner suddenly lost her temper and started breaking things?

♦♦♦♦♦♦♦♦♦♦♦♦♦♦

190. **W**hat if she started doing the above every six months or so? What if her anger were directed at you? Would it make a difference if she only yelled at you and wasn't physically abusive? What if she carried on in your presence but the attack wasn't targeted at you?

◆◆◆◆◆◆◆◆◆◆◆◆◆◆

191. *W*hat was the last emotion you felt overwhelmed by? What were the circumstances?

◆◆◆◆◆◆◆◆◆◆◆◆◆◆

192. *A*re you prone to any particular physical ailments (stomach pains, sore throats, gastrointestinal or genitourinary infections, or the like)?

◆◆◆◆◆◆◆◆◆◆◆◆◆◆

193. *H*ave you ever done anything to yourself that left
a physical scar? Do you believe you're the only one,
or do you think a lot of people hurt themselves?

◆◆◆◆◆◆◆◆◆◆◆◆◆◆

194. *D*o you ever feel especially vulnerable?

◆◆◆◆◆◆◆◆◆◆◆◆◆

195. *D*escribe the last time that you felt humiliated.

◆◆◆◆◆◆◆◆◆◆◆◆◆◆

196. *I*n what ways do you express your anger differently than your lover? How about your frustration?

◆◆◆◆◆◆◆◆◆◆◆◆◆

197. *I*f your lover raises her voice with you, does it mean that she is angry?

◆◆◆◆◆◆◆◆◆◆◆◆◆

198. *A*t times when your lover is angry but won't admit it, how do you know that she's angry? How do you respond?

◆◆◆◆◆◆◆◆◆◆◆◆◆◆

199. *I*f you and a close friend were both single, do you think it would ruin the friendship if you decided to have sex with each other? Would it matter if you agreed that it would happen only once?

◆◆◆◆◆◆◆◆◆◆◆◆◆◆

200. *D*o you believe you should only flirt with someone who you want to be lovers with?

◆◆◆◆◆◆◆◆◆◆◆◆◆◆

201. *I*f giving up the use of one of your limbs or one of your senses would ensure world peace, would you? If you could specify the loss, what would you choose to give up?

◆◆◆◆◆◆◆◆◆◆◆◆◆◆

202. *S*uppose your lover could learn an assortment of new sexual techniques by sleeping with another woman. Would you want her to do it? What if part of the deal was that you had to watch?

◆◆◆◆◆◆◆◆◆◆◆◆◆◆

203. *N*ame two ways that you want to be like your family of origin and two ways that you want to be different from them.

◆◆◆◆◆◆◆◆◆◆◆◆◆◆

204. *H*ave you ever thought that someone was deliberately withholding sex from you?

◆◆◆◆◆◆◆◆◆◆◆◆◆◆

205. *H*ave you ever deliberately withheld sex from your lover? Why or why not?

◆◆◆◆◆◆◆◆◆◆◆◆◆

206. **A** gree or disagree: Asking someone to dance is flirting.

◆◆◆◆◆◆◆◆◆◆◆◆◆

207. **W** hich would be more painful for you: having your lover leave you for a man or having her die?

◆◆◆◆◆◆◆◆◆◆◆◆◆

208. **D** o you find it hard to get close to another person?

♦♦♦♦♦♦♦♦♦♦♦♦♦♦

209. *I*f you sustained an injury that left you unable to be sexually stimulated, would you urge your lover to seek sex with someone else? Would it hurt you if she did?

♦♦♦♦♦♦♦♦♦♦♦♦♦♦

210. *I*f you lost all interest in sex, do you think your lover would stay with you? Would you expect her to?

◆◆◆◆◆◆◆◆◆◆◆◆◆◆

211. *H*ow much of a part do you think technique plays in sexual satisfaction?

◆◆◆◆◆◆◆◆◆◆◆◆◆◆

212. *N*ame three different sexual techniques.

◆◆◆◆◆◆◆◆◆◆◆◆◆

213. *H*ow many of these techniques have you discussed with your lover? Have you discussed them with anyone else?

◆◆◆◆◆◆◆◆◆◆◆◆◆◆

214. **D**o you feel safer talking about sex with your lover or with close friends?

◆◆◆◆◆◆◆◆◆◆◆◆◆◆

215. **D**o you believe that if a dyke is wearing leather it means that she or her partner is into S/M?

◆◆◆◆◆◆◆◆◆◆◆◆◆◆

216. **D**o you sometimes have trouble enjoying sex?

◆◆◆◆◆◆◆◆◆◆◆◆◆◆

217. **D**o you ever feel resentful that your lover doesn't understand you better?

◆◆◆◆◆◆◆◆◆◆◆◆◆◆

218. **A**re there aspects of your lover's personality that you don't understand and would like to know more about?

◆◆◆◆◆◆◆◆◆◆◆◆◆◆

219. **A**re there aspects of your lover's background that you don't understand and would like to know more about?

◆◆◆◆◆◆◆◆◆◆◆◆◆◆

220. **W**ould you say that you have ever had low self-esteem?

◆◆◆◆◆◆◆◆◆◆◆◆◆◆◆

221. **I**n relationships, what exactly qualifies for you as short-term and long-term?

◆◆◆◆◆◆◆◆◆◆◆◆◆◆

222. **D**o you find it harder to deal with emotional pain or physical pain?

◆◆◆◆◆◆◆◆◆◆◆◆◆◆◆

223. *I*f you had to choose between living with
recurring migraines or having your heart broken
again and again, which would you choose?

◆◆◆◆◆◆◆◆◆◆◆◆◆◆

224. *D*o you think that your friends believe that
your sex life is better than it actually is, or worse?

◆◆◆◆◆◆◆◆◆◆◆◆◆◆

225. **W**hat differences (spiritual, political, emotional, and so forth) would keep you from being in a long-term relationship with someone you were in love with?

◆◆◆◆◆◆◆◆◆◆◆◆◆◆

226. **I**f you did something thoughtless, would you rather that your lover become furious for a few hours or somewhat irritable for a few days? Why?

◆◆◆◆◆◆◆◆◆◆◆◆◆◆

227. *H*ave you ever wanted to end a relationship with someone, but still have sex with that person now and again?

◆◆◆◆◆◆◆◆◆◆◆◆◆◆

228. *I*f you had to spend one 24-hour period a month away from your lover, what would you do during that time? Do you think it would enhance your relationship?

◆◆◆◆◆◆◆◆◆◆◆◆◆◆

229. *I*f your lover has an interest that you don't share, do you try to become interested in it, fake interest, encourage her to do it without you, or something else?

◆◆◆◆◆◆◆◆◆◆◆◆◆◆

230. *I*f you discovered that your lover had a brief affair early in your relationship, how would you feel? How would it affect your relationship?

◆◆◆◆◆◆◆◆◆◆◆◆◆◆

231. *H*ave you and your lover ever discussed
the possibility of having affairs?

◆◆◆◆◆◆◆◆◆◆◆◆◆◆

232. *D*o you believe that the more you love someone,
the more they can hurt you?

◆◆◆◆◆◆◆◆◆◆◆◆◆◆

233. *W*ould you date someone of another race? Do
you think interracial relationships are more difficult?

◆◆◆◆◆◆◆◆◆◆◆◆◆◆

234. **W**ould you rather have a lover with an average face and a beautiful body, or an average body and a beautiful face?

◆◆◆◆◆◆◆◆◆◆◆◆◆

235. **H**ow would you react if your lover tested positive for HIV? Would it matter to you how she contracted the disease?

◆◆◆◆◆◆◆◆◆◆◆◆◆

236. **T**rue or false: People have to work to stay together.

◆◆◆◆◆◆◆◆◆◆◆◆◆◆

237. **W**hat was the worst heartbreak that you ever experienced? Did it affect your ability to trust?

◆◆◆◆◆◆◆◆◆◆◆◆◆◆

238. **D**o you suffer from chronic headaches?

◆◆◆◆◆◆◆◆◆◆◆◆◆◆

239. **H**ave you ever used your feelings of responsibility toward your lover as an excuse to keep you from doing something that you were afraid to do? Have you ever used these responsibilities to motivate you to do something you were afraid to do?

◆◆◆◆◆◆◆◆◆◆◆◆◆◆

240. *C*onsidering all the differences between you and your lover, which difference do you value the most? Which difference do you consider the most problematic?

◆◆◆◆◆◆◆◆◆◆◆◆◆◆

241. *W*hich do you enjoy more: the process of discovering what your partner enjoys sexually or the familiarity of already knowing what she likes?

◆◆◆◆◆◆◆◆◆◆◆◆◆◆

242. **D**o you think that you could fall in love with someone you aren't sexually attracted to?

◆◆◆◆◆◆◆◆◆◆◆◆◆◆

243. **C**ould you be sexually attracted to someone you aren't in love with?

◆◆◆◆◆◆◆◆◆◆◆◆◆◆

244. **I**f you could have any one person's love and desire forever, would you take it? If so, whom would you pick? Why?

◆◆◆◆◆◆◆◆◆◆◆◆◆

245. **D**o you sometimes feel that you should be enjoying sex more?

◆◆◆◆◆◆◆◆◆◆◆◆◆

246. **D**o you believe lovers should depend upon each other?

◆◆◆◆◆◆◆◆◆◆◆◆◆

247. **D**o you believe true love conquers all?

◆◆◆◆◆◆◆◆◆◆◆◆◆◆

248. **W**hich of you is better at keeping an important issue at bay when the time or place is inappropriate for dealing with it?

◆◆◆◆◆◆◆◆◆◆◆◆◆◆

249. **H**ave you ever spied on a lover you didn't trust? What happened?

◆◆◆◆◆◆◆◆◆◆◆◆◆◆

250. *W*hat gives you the most intense orgasms: oral sex, masturbation, digital stimulation, or something else?

◆◆◆◆◆◆◆◆◆◆◆◆◆◆

251. *I*f you had to give up all but one of the above, which would you keep?

◆◆◆◆◆◆◆◆◆◆◆◆◆◆

252. *W*hat is the most giving, humanitarian thing you have ever done for another person? Were you in love with that person?

◆◆◆◆◆◆◆◆◆◆◆◆◆◆◆◆

253. *I*f you knew you would die today, how long would you want your lover to wait before starting a new relationship? How long would you wait if the situation were reversed?

◆◆◆◆◆◆◆◆◆◆◆◆◆◆◆◆

254. *I*f your lover were going through an intense personal crisis and wanted to live by herself for six months, would you feel it marked the beginning of the end of your relationship? Why or why not?

◆◆◆◆◆◆◆◆◆◆◆◆◆◆◆

255. *I*f you were going through an intense personal crisis and
could afford to live apart from your lover, would you do so?
Why or why not?

◆◆◆◆◆◆◆◆◆◆◆◆◆◆◆

256. *S*ince becoming sexually active, what is the longest time
you have gone without sex? Was it by choice?

◆◆◆◆◆◆◆◆◆◆◆◆◆◆

257. *D*o you believe that celibacy is ever a choice, or
always a state forced by outside circumstances?

◆◆◆◆◆◆◆◆◆◆◆◆◆◆◆

258. **D**o you believe that your lover and your soul mate are always the same person? Would you prefer them to be the same person? Why or why not?

◆◆◆◆◆◆◆◆◆◆◆◆◆◆

259. **H**ow much of your delight in sex comes from pleasuring your partner?

◆◆◆◆◆◆◆◆◆◆◆◆◆

260. **I**f you had to give up either giving or receiving sexually, which would you choose to do without? Why?

◆◆◆◆◆◆◆◆◆◆◆◆◆◆

261. *H*ave you ever discussed sexuality with someone you considered to be elderly? If so, what was the best thing about the discussion?

◆◆◆◆◆◆◆◆◆◆◆◆◆◆

262. *D*o you think you will ever reach an age when you are too old to fall in love?

◆◆◆◆◆◆◆◆◆◆◆◆◆◆

263. *I*f you became intensely unhappy and dissatisfied with your partner, would you be more likely to end the relationship or to have an affair? Which would you prefer your lover do if the situation were reversed?

◆◆◆◆◆◆◆◆◆◆◆◆◆◆

264. *W*ould you like to read old love letters written to your lover by a previous lover? Why or why not? Would you read letters that your lover wrote to other lovers?

◆◆◆◆◆◆◆◆◆◆◆◆◆◆

265. *H*ow would you react if your lover were arrested and charged with a serious crime? What if she admitted to you that she did it?

◆◆◆◆◆◆◆◆◆◆◆◆◆

266. *W*hat is the best discovery you have made about your lover since you first got together?

◆◆◆◆◆◆◆◆◆◆◆◆

267. *W*hen and where do you make love most often?

◆◆◆◆◆◆◆◆◆◆◆◆◆

268. *H*ow do you feel when you find yourself attracted to a woman that your friends neither like nor approve of? Would you rather that your friends share their opinions with you or keep them to themselves?

◆◆◆◆◆◆◆◆◆◆◆◆◆

269. *W*ould you be willing to spend six months separated from your lover if it meant you could have all the money you ever wanted?

◆◆◆◆◆◆◆◆◆◆◆◆◆◆◆

270. **I**n what ways do you feel you and your partner get along better than other couples you know? In what ways do you think you and your lover get along worse?

◆◆◆◆◆◆◆◆◆◆◆◆◆◆

271. **I**f you fell in love with a woman who said that she'd be your lover *only* if you had an open relationship, would you be willing? What sort of rules, requirements, or boundaries would you want to set?

◆◆◆◆◆◆◆◆◆◆◆◆◆◆◆

272. **W**ould it be harder for you to deal with your lover leaving you for another woman or for a man? Why?

◆◆◆◆◆◆◆◆◆◆◆◆◆◆◆

273. **D**o you think there is a point at which love becomes so overwhelming that it is unhealthy?

◆◆◆◆◆◆◆◆◆◆◆◆◆◆◆

274. **I**f you could change the time or place that you usually make love, what changes would you make?

✦✦✦✦✦✦✦✦✦✦✦✦✦

275. **W**ho among the couples that you know has the best relationship? What appeals to you the most about their relationship?

✦✦✦✦✦✦✦✦✦✦✦✦✦

276. **W**hat is your definition of commitment?
What is the scariest thing about making a commitment?
What is the most rewarding thing about making a commitment?

◆◆◆◆◆◆◆◆◆◆◆◆◆◆

277. *I*f you fell in love with someone who would not make a commitment to you, would you get involved anyway?

◆◆◆◆◆◆◆◆◆◆◆◆◆◆

278. *S*uppose you had to choose between being with someone who was totally committed to you but had trouble controlling her temper, or someone who refused to commit to you but always treated you with tenderness and respect. Who would you choose?

♦♦♦♦♦♦♦♦♦♦♦♦♦♦

279. *N*ame one nonsexual thing that your partner does that makes you feel the most loved.

♦♦♦♦♦♦♦♦♦♦♦♦♦♦

280. *N*ame one important lesson you've learned from a breakup.

♦♦♦♦♦♦♦♦♦♦♦♦♦♦

281. *D*o you feel an obligation to continue contact with a former lover? Why or why not?

◆◆◆◆◆◆◆◆◆◆◆◆◆◆◆

282. *H*ow would you feel if a former lover explained that she was having difficulty with continued contact and asked that you let her initiate all contact for a while? Would you do it? Why or why not?

◆◆◆◆◆◆◆◆◆◆◆◆◆◆

283. *H*ave you ever pretended that you were enjoying sex more than you actually were? If so, what were the circumstances?

◆◆◆◆◆◆◆◆◆◆◆◆◆◆

284. *I*f you had the power to make any one person gay, would you use it? Who would you choose?

◆◆◆◆◆◆◆◆◆◆◆◆◆

285. *D*escribe the last time when you got very angry about something and vented your anger on your lover. How did she react? How would you have preferred her to react?

◆◆◆◆◆◆◆◆◆◆◆◆◆

286. *I*f you won a lottery, how would it change your life?

♦♦♦♦♦♦♦♦♦♦♦♦♦♦

287. *I*f you and your lover started to have sexual problems, would you search for some underlying cause in yourself or in your lover, or would you simply try to find practical ways to solve the problems?

♦♦♦♦♦♦♦♦♦♦♦♦♦♦

288. *I*f you were dying and could leave only one thing to your lover, what would it be? What would she want to get?

◆◆◆◆◆◆◆◆◆◆◆◆◆◆

289. *H*ave you ever displayed affection for your lover in a public place? What were the circumstances? What is the strongest display of public affection you have ever witnessed? How did you feel about it?

◆◆◆◆◆◆◆◆◆◆◆◆◆◆

290. *H*ow has the role of romance changed in your life over the years?

◆◆◆◆◆◆◆◆◆◆◆◆◆◆◆

291. **W**ould you like more romance in your life?
What steps could you take to have more romance in your life?

◆◆◆◆◆◆◆◆◆◆◆◆◆◆◆

292. **D**oes your partner ever say that you don't listen to her?

◆◆◆◆◆◆◆◆◆◆◆◆◆◆◆

293. **D**oes your partner ever tell you that you don't express yourself enough to her?

◆◆◆◆◆◆◆◆◆◆◆◆◆◆

294. *W*ould you watch a video of yourself
making love? Would you make such a video?
Why or why not?

◆◆◆◆◆◆◆◆◆◆◆◆◆

295. *I*f you are very attracted to someone, and another person
expresses an interest in her, too, does this strengthen your interest
or diminish it?

◆◆◆◆◆◆◆◆◆◆◆◆◆◆

296. *H*ave you ever refused to communicate with someone
you were once close to? If so, did you explain your
behavior, or just refuse to communicate? What is the worst
thing you have ever done to someone close to you?

◆◆◆◆◆◆◆◆◆◆◆◆◆◆

297. *W*hat do you think determines sexual orientation?
Nature? Nurture? Biology? Environment? Choice?

◆◆◆◆◆◆◆◆◆◆◆◆◆◆

298. *A*re you sexually adventurous or timid?

◆◆◆◆◆◆◆◆◆◆◆◆◆◆

299. *D*o you initiate new sexual techniques or positions?

◆◆◆◆◆◆◆◆◆◆◆◆◆◆

300. *A*re you willing to try new things as long as someone else does the initiating?

◆◆◆◆◆◆◆◆◆◆◆◆◆◆

301. *I*f you had to choose to either halve or double
your sex drive, which would you choose?

♦♦♦♦♦♦♦♦♦♦♦♦♦♦

302. *A*re there times when you feel guilty, embarrassed, or ashamed during or just after sex? Do you know why?

♦♦♦♦♦♦♦♦♦♦♦♦♦

303. *H*ave you ever cried during or just after sex? Do you know why?

♦♦♦♦♦♦♦♦♦♦♦♦♦

304. *D*id you ever feel guilty or ashamed about sex when you were younger, or with past lovers?

◆◆◆◆◆◆◆◆◆◆◆◆◆◆

305. **W**ould you prefer to have a wild, passionate relationship or a steady, reliable one?

◆◆◆◆◆◆◆◆◆◆◆◆◆◆

306. **S**uppose that you are single and a former lover is having problems in her relationship. Would you tell her if you were still interested in a relationship with her?

◆◆◆◆◆◆◆◆◆◆◆◆◆◆

307. **D**o you prefer predictable sex or unpredictable sex?

◆◆◆◆◆◆◆◆◆◆◆◆◆◆

308. *S*uppose your lover went out of town and ended up having a fling with an old flame. Would you want to be told? Would it matter if your lover promised never to see the other woman again? Would an admission of infidelity change your relationship? If so, in what way? If you were the one who had the fling, would you tell your lover? Why or why not?

◆◆◆◆◆◆◆◆◆◆◆◆◆◆

309. *I*f you came upon two teenagers making love in the woods, would you watch?

◆◆◆◆◆◆◆◆◆◆◆◆◆◆

310. *H*ave you ever tried to stop yourself from falling in love? If so, describe the circumstances.

◆◆◆◆◆◆◆◆◆◆◆◆◆◆

311. *I*f you could safely change any part of your body, what body part would you change and why?

◆◆◆◆◆◆◆◆◆◆◆◆◆◆

312. **W**ould it bother you more to discover that your lover has had a brief sexual encounter with someone else, or that she regularly fantasizes about another person? Why?

◆◆◆◆◆◆◆◆◆◆◆◆◆◆

313. **I**f a close friend told you that she saw your lover having a romantic lunch with a woman, but your lover denied it, whom would you believe? How much evidence would it take for you to concede that your lover was lying to you?

◆◆◆◆◆◆◆◆◆◆◆◆◆◆

314. *H*ave you ever gone back to a person after having
the relationship end? Why? What happened?
Have you ever taken anyone back?

◆◆◆◆◆◆◆◆◆◆◆◆◆◆

315. *I*f someone dumped you and a month later wanted
to get back together with you, would you let her?
Why or why not?

◆◆◆◆◆◆◆◆◆◆◆◆◆◆

316. *S*uppose it has been a year since a lover left you, and though you are dating, you are not in a serious relationship. How would you react if your ex-lover wanted to get back together with you?

◆◆◆◆◆◆◆◆◆◆◆◆◆◆

317. *S*uppose your lover told you that she would be either *sexually* monogamous with you or *emotionally* monogamous with you, but not both.
Which would you want her to be?

♦♦♦♦♦♦♦♦♦♦♦♦♦♦♦

318. **D**o you ever have feelings of care, concern, and love for more than one person at a time?

♦♦♦♦♦♦♦♦♦♦♦♦♦♦♦

319. **H**ow many times in your life have you felt that you were in love?

♦♦♦♦♦♦♦♦♦♦♦♦♦♦♦

320. **H**ave you ever been in love with more than one person at the same time? If so, how did you handle that? How did they?

◆◆◆◆◆◆◆◆◆◆◆◆◆◆

321. *H*ave you ever loved someone whom you didn't respect? If so, did it cause you to respect yourself less?

◆◆◆◆◆◆◆◆◆◆◆◆◆◆

322. *H*ave you ever had sex with more than one person at a time? If so, what did you like or dislike about it? Were they the same sex?

◆◆◆◆◆◆◆◆◆◆◆◆◆◆

323. *W*ould you like to have an increased sense of independence or togetherness in your relationship?

◆◆◆◆◆◆◆◆◆◆◆◆◆◆

324. **W**hile you and your lover are on a vacation, you meet a friendly, wealthy couple, and the four of you enjoy a fantastic dinner together. That night, they approach you and offer to pay you $20,000 in cash if you will join them for a threesome. Would you do it? What if you couldn't tell your lover until afterwards? What if it were a heterosexual couple?

◆◆◆◆◆◆◆◆◆◆◆◆◆◆

325. **H**ave you ever been in love with someone and never told the person how you felt? If so, why? What was hardest about it?

◆◆◆◆◆◆◆◆◆◆◆◆◆◆

326. **W**ould you rather have a passionate relationship with a woman with whom you share few interests and beliefs, or a less passionate relationship with a woman with whom you share much in common?

◆◆◆◆◆◆◆◆◆◆◆◆◆◆

327. **W**hat things, other than physical contact, arouse you sexually? (For example, pictures, books, movies, phone sex, something else?)

◆◆◆◆◆◆◆◆◆◆◆◆◆◆

328. *H*ave you ever seen or read any lesbian-made erotica?
If so, do you find it different from the lesbian erotica made
by heterosexuals?

◆◆◆◆◆◆◆◆◆◆◆◆◆◆

329. *I*f a fantastic lifetime career opportunity came up for your
lover involving a move to another country, would you urge
her to take it? Would you move with her? Suppose that you
couldn't join her there for two years. Would you remain
faithful and expect her to do the same?

◆◆◆◆◆◆◆◆◆◆◆◆◆◆

330. **W**ere you ever in a long-distance relationship?
If so, what was good about it? What was bad about it?

◆◆◆◆◆◆◆◆◆◆◆◆◆◆

331. **W**hat's the longest amount of time you've spent away
from your current lover? How about other lovers?

◆◆◆◆◆◆◆◆◆◆◆◆◆◆

332. **I**f you had to make love in total darkness
or in total silence, which would you choose?

◆◆◆◆◆◆◆◆◆◆◆◆◆◆◆

333. *H*ave you ever had a commitment ceremony or a bonding ritual with a lover? If so, was it a public one, with friends and family?

◆◆◆◆◆◆◆◆◆◆◆◆◆◆◆

334. *D*o you feel that a ceremony, public or private, is something that you'd like to do?

◆◆◆◆◆◆◆◆◆◆◆◆◆◆◆

335. *H*ave you ever had a lover who didn't share some of your important beliefs? How did the relationship work out?

◆◆◆◆◆◆◆◆◆◆◆◆◆◆◆

336. *W*hen you first fall in love, do you focus all your attention on that person? Do you think this is a normal part of being in love or that it creates an unhealthy dependence on the person?

◆◆◆◆◆◆◆◆◆◆◆◆◆◆

337. *N*ame one thing that your parents did that you swore as a child you would never do, but that you do now.

◆◆◆◆◆◆◆◆◆◆◆◆◆◆

338. *I*s there anything your parents did that you are glad you now do?

◆◆◆◆◆◆◆◆◆◆◆◆◆◆

339. **W**hen you fall in love, do you find that you take on your lover's friends? Do you still retain your own friends?

◆◆◆◆◆◆◆◆◆◆◆◆◆◆

340. **Y**ou have decided that you no longer want to deal with one of your lover's friends. Will you allow time and space for your lover to continue the friendship if she wants to? Would you try to influence your lover to give up the friend? Would you resent any time that she may spend with the friend? Would you resent the friend?

◆◆◆◆◆◆◆◆◆◆◆◆◆◆

341. *H*ave you ever called a lover by an ex-lover's name or vice versa? If so, how did that feel? How did your lover react?

◆◆◆◆◆◆◆◆◆◆◆◆◆◆

342. *H*ow do you express your resentment? How does your lover express her resentment?

◆◆◆◆◆◆◆◆◆◆◆◆◆

343. *W*hat's the longest that you have stayed extremely angry?

◆◆◆◆◆◆◆◆◆◆◆◆◆◆

344. **W**hen was the last time you had to physically remove yourself
from a situation with your lover before you could deal with it?
When that happens, what do you use that space for?
How is the situation better after you return?

◆◆◆◆◆◆◆◆◆◆◆◆◆◆

345. **W**hat is your favorite book? Why?

♦♦♦♦♦♦♦♦♦♦♦♦♦♦

346. *I*f you could finally get your lover to sit and watch that one movie with you that she has been avoiding, what would it be? Why do you think she has resisted watching it?

♦♦♦♦♦♦♦♦♦♦♦♦♦♦

347. *W*hich of your past relationships would you say was the best and which would you say was the worst? Why?

◆◆◆◆◆◆◆◆◆◆◆◆◆◆◆

348. **D**o you ever feel that you often don't have time enough for yourself? When you get time alone for yourself, what do you like to do? Do you ever make a point of setting time aside to do something for yourself? If so, how often? When was the last time?

◆◆◆◆◆◆◆◆◆◆◆◆◆◆◆

349. **H**ow often do you let the needs and wants of your lover or friends take priority over your own? When was the last time?

◆◆◆◆◆◆◆◆◆◆◆◆◆◆◆

350. **W**ould you be insulted if a potential partner asked you to get tested for HIV? Would you get tested?

◆◆◆◆◆◆◆◆◆◆◆◆◆◆◆

351. **H**ave you ever wondered if you were abused as a child?

◆◆◆◆◆◆◆◆◆◆◆◆◆◆

352. **D**o you get confused about whom to trust, or end up trusting the wrong people?

♦♦♦♦♦♦♦♦♦♦♦♦♦♦

353. **N**ame the last thing that happened to you that really bummed you out.

♦♦♦♦♦♦♦♦♦♦♦♦♦♦

354. **D**o you think butch and femme identities mimic heterosexual culture?

♦♦♦♦♦♦♦♦♦♦♦♦♦

355. **D**escribe the last time that you dropped everything or went out of your way to help a friend.

◆◆◆◆◆◆◆◆◆◆◆◆◆◆

356. **D**o you think that your lover should know
when you feel that something is hurtful?

◆◆◆◆◆◆◆◆◆◆◆◆◆◆

357. **D**o you always know how your lover is feeling?

◆◆◆◆◆◆◆◆◆◆◆◆◆◆

358. **D**o you believe that failing to say what is true
can be as much of a lie as saying things that are untrue?

♦♦♦♦♦♦♦♦♦♦♦♦♦♦

359. ***B***etween you and your lover, what is considered to be "grounds for divorce"?

♦♦♦♦♦♦♦♦♦♦♦♦♦♦

360. ***D***o you ever panic and lie without thinking?

♦♦♦♦♦♦♦♦♦♦♦♦♦

361. ***I***s lying ever justifiable? If so, when?

◆◆◆◆◆◆◆◆◆◆◆◆◆◆◆

362. ***H***ave you ever faked an orgasm?
If so, when and why?

◆◆◆◆◆◆◆◆◆◆◆◆◆◆◆

363. ***H***ave you ever lied to protect
the feelings of another person?

◆◆◆◆◆◆◆◆◆◆◆◆◆◆

364. ***T***rue or false: I respect long-term relationships.

◆◆◆◆◆◆◆◆◆◆◆◆◆◆

365. **H**as a lover or a friend ever used against you
something that you told them in confidence?

◆◆◆◆◆◆◆◆◆◆◆◆◆◆

366. **W**hat is your favorite movie? Why?

◆◆◆◆◆◆◆◆◆◆◆◆◆◆

367. **H**ow would you feel about entering into a relationship with a
woman who has children? Would you do it? Why or why not?

◆◆◆◆◆◆◆◆◆◆◆◆◆◆◆

368. **D**o either you or your lover drink alcohol?
Name one good thing about it and one bad thing.
Has drinking ever caused problems in your relationship?

◆◆◆◆◆◆◆◆◆◆◆◆◆◆◆

369. **W**ould you hesitate to get involved with a woman who is totally out of the closet? How about a woman who is totally in the closet?

◆◆◆◆◆◆◆◆◆◆◆◆◆◆

370. **D**o you believe part of really loving someone
is knowing when to leave?

◆◆◆◆◆◆◆◆◆◆◆◆◆◆

371. **N**ame the lesbian whom you most admire. Why?

◆◆◆◆◆◆◆◆◆◆◆◆◆◆

372. **D**escribe your best and worst experience
during high school.

◆◆◆◆◆◆◆◆◆◆◆◆◆◆

373. *H*ow often do you have contact with your family?
Is it quality contact?

◆◆◆◆◆◆◆◆◆◆◆◆◆◆

374. *D*o you find a change in plans
more jarring than interesting?

◆◆◆◆◆◆◆◆◆◆◆◆◆◆

375. *W*ould you describe your
belief system as flexible or firm?

♦♦♦♦♦♦♦♦♦♦♦♦♦♦♦

376. **D**o you think that your responsibilities to your lover keep you from doing things that you might otherwise like to do? Like what?

♦♦♦♦♦♦♦♦♦♦♦♦♦♦♦

377. **I**f you and your lover could have an all-expenses-paid vacation for up to a month, where would you go? What if only one of you could go?

◆◆◆◆◆◆◆◆◆◆◆◆◆◆

378. **A**re there specific aspects of your relationship that you would expect your lover to never mention to anyone?

◆◆◆◆◆◆◆◆◆◆◆◆◆◆

379. **D**escribe the last time that you solved an issue by maintaining a friendly tone rather than a confrontational tone.

◆◆◆◆◆◆◆◆◆◆◆◆◆◆

380. **H**ave you ever been in a relationship that was physically, psychologically, emotionally, or sexually abusive?

◆◆◆◆◆◆◆◆◆◆◆◆◆◆

381. *I*f you had to categorize each of your friends
and ex-lovers as butch or femme, what would each be?
How about yourself? Is your categorization based more
on temperament or on physical appearance?

◆◆◆◆◆◆◆◆◆◆◆◆◆◆

382. *D*o you have any issues with your lover that
you think would be better handled through
direct confrontation?

◆◆◆◆◆◆◆◆◆◆◆◆◆◆

383. *W*ould you rather suffer an injury that left you
numb from the waist down or completely deaf?

◆◆◆◆◆◆◆◆◆◆◆◆◆◆

384. *D*o you often find yourself trying to smooth over an
uncomfortable situation? If so, why, do you think?
Have you ever regretted doing so? When?

◆◆◆◆◆◆◆◆◆◆◆◆◆◆

385. *W*hat is the longest time you have known a woman
before having sex with her? What is the shortest time?

◆◆◆◆◆◆◆◆◆◆◆◆◆◆

386. *I*f you had the chance to have up to twenty sessions
with a therapist for free, would you go? Why or why not?

◆◆◆◆◆◆◆◆◆◆◆◆◆

387. *I*f your lover had the same opportunity, would you want
her to pick the same therapist as you? Why or why not?

◆◆◆◆◆◆◆◆◆◆◆◆◆

388. *H*ave you ever gone out dressed in drag?
If so, what were the circumstances?

◆◆◆◆◆◆◆◆◆◆◆◆◆◆

389. **H**ave you had fun while answering these questions?

◆◆◆◆◆◆◆◆◆◆◆◆◆◆

390. **H**ave you been honest in answering these questions?

◆◆◆◆◆◆◆◆◆◆◆◆◆

391. **N**ame three things you've learned by answering these questions.

APPENDIX

Looking closely at the responses that you recorded to the following items might indicate that you need more information in the area of codependence: 5, 7, 10, 11, 12, 16, 26, 42, 53, 55, 74, 75, 76, 77, 87, 89, 90, 93, 101, 102, 104, 106, 107, 135, 136, 137, 138, 142, 146, 147, 150, 152, 153, 156, 162, 169, 170, 174, 175, 177, 178, 179, 180, 181, 183, 188, 189, 190, 191, 192, 194, 195, 197, 204, 205, 206, 217, 220, 222, 228, 230, 232, 238, 239, 245, 246, 247, 249, 254, 256, 258, 264, 268, 269, 273, 283, 285, 287, 296, 308, 311, 313, 316, 323, 325, 329, 331, 336, 339, 340, 344, 348, 349, 352, 355, 356, 357, 360, 361, 362, 368 370, 374, 376, 378, 380, 384.

Looking closely at the responses that you recorded to the following items might indicate that you need more information in the area of child abuse: 43, 90, 93, 94, 96, 97, 98, 99, 101, 103, 119, 129, 135, 136, 137, 138, 140, 141, 142, 144, 156, 162, 189, 190, 191, 192, 193, 194, 195, 197, 204, 205, 208, 216, 220, 222, 232, 238, 245, 273, 299, 302, 303, 304, 311, 339, 344, 351, 352, 360, 361, 368, 378, 380.

Looking closely at the responses that you recorded to the following items might indicate that you need more information in the area of childhood sexual abuse: 30, 31, 32, 36, 38, 42, 43, 57, 62, 64, 90, 129, 135, 136, 137, 138, 142, 144, 156, 189, 191, 192, 193, 194, 195, 204, 205, 208, 216, 220, 222, 238, 245, 273, 283, 298, 302, 303, 304, 308, 311, 344, 351, 352, 360, 361, 368, 378, 380.